50
A Couples Journal

QUESTIONS FOR A DEEPER CONNECTION.

©The Life Graduate Publishing Group

The Life Graduate
PUBLISHING GROUP

ABOUT THE COUPLE

Partner 1
Name: _____

Partner 2
Name:_____

When You first starting dating _____

Name   Name

Partner 1   **Partner 2**
Age :   Age :

50 Questions for a Deeper Connection

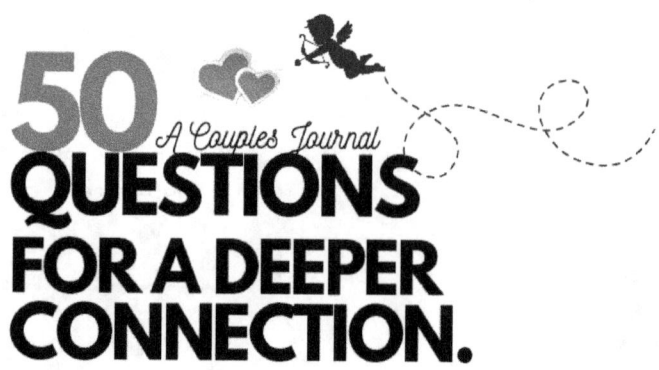

50 QUESTIONS FOR A DEEPER CONNECTION.

A Couples Journal

ABOUT THE JOURNAL

This Journal has been designed so you can learn more about your partner and develop a deeper connection with them.

50 Questions For A Deeper Connection will open up discussions between you and your partner that will strengthen your bond and relationship.

This journal has been split into 3 sections:

Section 1: Partner 1 Story and Answers
Section 2: Partner 2 Story and Answers
Section 3: Your Journey Together

50
A Couples Journal

QUESTIONS FOR A DEEPER CONNECTION.

SECTION 1 – PARTNER 1

It's time to answer your questions!

Getting to Know You

#1 What have you been told about you as a baby?

_____

_____

_____

_____

_____

_____

#2 Were you in good health as a baby?

_____

_____

_____

#3 Did you have any unique characteristics or funny things you did as a baby?

_____

_____

_____

_____

The Young Years

#4 What are your fondest memories growing up between the ages of 5 years to 12 years?

_____

_____

_____

_____

_____

_____

_____

_____

_____

_____

The Young Years Continued...

#5 Where did you grow up as a child?
(House, location, town etc)

_____

_____

_____

#6 Who was your best friend or your best friends as a kid?

_____

_____

#7 What was your favorite day of the week and why?

_____

_____

_____

The Young Years Continued...

#8 What did you want to be when you were a child?

_____

#9 What elementary/primary school did you go to and where was it located?

_____

_____

#10 Describe your most memorable moment or story from school.

_____

_____

_____

_____

_____

_____

_____

_____

The Young Years Continued...

#11   What was your favorite toy growing up?

_____

_____

#12   Did you have a pet or any pets?

_____

_____

#13   What was your favorite T.V show to watch as a kid?

_____

_____

#14   Was there a moment you remember getting into big trouble as a child? Was there a punishment?

_____

_____

_____

_____

_____

Teenage Years

#15 Did you date anyone as a teenager and if so, for how long?

_____

_____

#16 What is your most memorable moment as a teenager?

_____

_____

_____

_____

#17 If you knew what you know today, what would you have done differently as a teenager?

_____

_____

_____

_____

Teenage Years

#18 Who was in your friendship group in your late teens?

_____

_____

_____

_____

_____

#19 Did you have any nicknames?

_____

_____

#20 What 5 words come to mind to describe your teenage years?

1. _____

2. _____

3. _____

4. _____

5. _____

When I was….

#21 When I was in my final year of Elementary/Primary School, I was perhaps best known for....

_____

_____

#22 When I was 12 yrs old, I wanted to be a......

_____

#23 When I was a teenager, I had a crush on.....

_____

#24 When I was 17 years old, my favorite music and band was..

_____

#25 When I was in 18, the thing I wish I had more than anything else was...

_____

_____

#26 When I was young, I loved to travel to.......

_____

_____

When I was....

#27 When I was 18 yrs, I had a reputation for....

_____

_____

#28 When I was in my teens, the biggest news story that stands out to me was.....

_____

_____

_____

#29 When I was growing up, the 3 favorite movies I remember watching were:

1. _____

2. _____

3. _____

Deep & Meaningful

#30 I wish I had the opportunity to...

_____

_____

_____

#31 The quote that resonates most with me is..

_____

_____

_____

_____

#32 If there is one thing I would like to be known for, it would be:

_____

_____

_____

_____

#33 Not many people know this about me, so let me share it with you:

_____

_____

_____

_____

_____

_____

_____

#34 The activity or hobby that I enjoy most to do now is.....

_____

_____

#35 I have the unique ability to be able to....

_____

_____

_____

Deep &
Meaningful

#36   If I was able to go back to a special time in my life, it would be...

_____

_____

_____

#37   If I was to pass on one word of advice to others, it would be..

_____

_____

_____

#38   There are special moments in life that you wish you could pause to enjoy for longer. Mine would be......

_____

_____

_____

_____

#39 When I look back on my life so far, my 3 proudest moments are:

1 _____

2 _____

3 _____

#40 If there were 3 famous people that I could have dinner with, they would be:

1 _____

2 _____

3 _____

I think you need to know this!

#41   When I first laid eyes on you, I felt....

_____
_____
_____

#42   The thing I love to do with you most is.....

_____
_____
_____

#43   If I ever need cheering up, the way you could help me would be to.....

_____
_____
_____

#44   These are the qualities that I see in you that make you very special to me.

_____
_____
_____
_____

I think you need to know this!

#45   When I close my eyes and think about you, this is what first comes to mind....

_____

_____

#46   If you were to take me somewhere special, it would be...

_____

_____

_____

#47   My perfect day with you would look like this....

_____

_____

_____

_____

_____

_____

#48   Intimacy & Romance:
      This is what they mean to me...

_____

_____

_____

_____

#49 If I was given $10,000 right now, I would........

_____

_____

_____

_____

#50 A loving relationship to me is.....

_____

_____

_____

_____

_____

_____

_____

_____

The final word..

There have been many questions that I have answered in this journal, but I would also like to share this with you...

Your time to write anything else you wish to share

_____

_____

_____

_____

_____

_____

_____

_____

_____

Notes

Notes

Notes

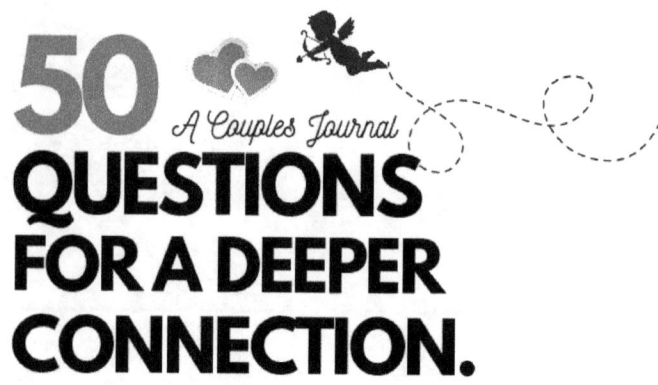

50
A Couples Journal
QUESTIONS
FOR A DEEPER
CONNECTION.

SECTION 2 - PARTNER 2

It's time to answer your questions!

Getting to Know You

#1 What have you been told about you as a baby?

_____

_____

_____

_____

_____

#2 Were you in good health as a baby?

_____

_____

_____

#3 Did you have any unique characteristics or funny things you did as a baby?

_____

_____

_____

_____

The Young Years

#4 What are your fondest memories growing up between the ages of 5 years to 12 years?

_____

_____

_____

_____

_____

_____

_____

_____

_____

_____

The Young Years Continued...

#5 Where did you grow up as a child?
(House, location, town etc)

_____

_____

_____

_____

#6 Who was your best friend or your best friends as a kid?

_____

_____

#7 What was your favorite day of the week and why?

_____

_____

_____

_____

The Young Years Continued...

#8 What did you want to be when you were a child?

_____

#9 What elementary/primary school did you go to and where was it located?

_____

_____

#10 Describe your most memorable moment or story from school.

_____

_____

_____

_____

_____

_____

_____

_____

_____

The Young Years Continued...

#11   What was your favorite toy growing up?

_____

_____

#12   Did you have a pet or any pets?

_____

_____

#13   What was your favorite T.V show to watch as a kid?

_____

_____

#14   Was there a moment you remember getting into big trouble as a child? Was there a punishment?

_____

_____

_____

_____

_____

Teenage Years

#15 Did you date anyone as a teenager and if so, for how long?

_____

_____

#16 What is your most memorable moment as a teenager?

_____

_____

_____

_____

#17 If you knew what you know today, what would you have done differently as a teenager?

_____

_____

_____

_____

Teenage Years

#18 Who was in your friendship group in your late teens?

_____

_____

_____

_____

_____

#19 Did you have any nicknames?

_____

_____

#20 What 5 words come to mind to describe your teenage years?

1. _____

2. _____

3. _____

4. _____

5. _____

When I was....

#21 When I was in my final year of Elementary/Primary School, I was perhaps best known for....

_____

_____

#22 When I was 12 yrs old, I wanted to be a......

_____

#23 When I was a teenager, I had a crush on.....

_____

#24 When I was 17 years old, my favorite music and band was..

_____

#25 When I was in 18, the thing I wish I had more than anything else was...

_____

_____

#26 When I was young, I loved to travel to.......

_____

_____

When I was....

#27   When I was 18 yrs, I had a reputation for....

_____

_____

#28   When I was in my teens, the biggest news story that stands out to me was.....

_____

_____

_____

#29   When I was growing up, the 3 favorite movies I remember watching were:

1. _____

2. _____

3. _____

Deep & Meaningful

#30   I wish I had the opportunity to...

_____

_____

_____

#31   The quote that resonates most with me is..

_____

_____

_____

#32   If there is one thing I would like to be known for, it would be:

_____

_____

_____

_____

#33 Not many people know this about me, so let me share it with you:

_____

_____

_____

_____

_____

_____

_____

#34 The activity or hobby that I enjoy most to do now is.....

_____

_____

#35 I have the unique ability to be able to....

_____

_____

_____

Deep & Meaningful

#36 If I was able to go back to a special time in my life, it would be...

_____

_____

_____

#37 If I was to pass on one word of advice to others, it would be..

_____

_____

_____

#38 There are special moments in life that you wish you could pause to enjoy for longer. Mine would be......

_____

_____

_____

_____

Deep & Meaningful

#39 When I look back on my life so far, my 3 proudest moments are:

1 _____

2 _____

3 _____

#40 If there were 3 famous people that I could have dinner with, they would be:

1 _____

2 _____

3 _____

I think you need to know this!

#41 When I first laid eyes on you, I felt....

_____

_____

_____

#42 The thing I love to do with you most is.....

_____

_____

_____

#43 If I ever need cheering up, the way you could help me would be to.....

_____

_____

_____

#44 These are the qualities that I see in you that make you very special to me.

_____

_____

_____

_____

I think you need to know this!

#45   When I close my eyes and think about you, this is what first comes to mind....

_____

_____

#46   If you were to take me somewhere special, it would be...

_____

_____

_____

#47   My perfect day with you would look like this....

_____

_____

_____

_____

_____

_____

#48   Intimacy & Romance:
This is what they mean to me...

_____

_____

_____

_____

#49   If I was given $10,000 right now, I would........

_____

_____

_____

_____

#50   A loving relationship to me is.....

_____

_____

_____

_____

_____

_____

_____

_____

The final word..

There have been many questions that I have answered in this journal, but I would also like to share this with you...

Your time to write anything else you wish to share

_____

_____

_____

_____

_____

_____

_____

_____

_____

_____

_____

Notes

Notes

50 **A Couples Journal**
QUESTIONS
FOR A DEEPER
CONNECTION.

SECTION 3

OUR JOURNEY TOGETHER

Add information in this section about your journey so far as a couple.

We first met at: (Location/date)

_____

_____

The first time we kissed was:

_____

_____

_____

Our first real travel adventure together was:

_____

_____

_____

_____

Complete this sentence: ' I can always rely on you to.....'
Partner 1:

_____

_____

_____

Partner 2:

_____

_____

_____

Our Journey

Photos, moments....anything

Our Journey

Photos, moments....anything

Our Journey

Photos, moments....anything

Our Journey

Photos, moments....anything

Our Journey

Photos, moments....anything

Our Journey

Photos, moments....anything

Our Journey

Photos, moments....anything

Our Journey

Photos, moments....anything

Notes

Notes

50 QUESTIONS FOR A DEEPER CONNECTION.

A Couples Journal